cool smoothies

juices and cocktails

cool smoothies

juices and cocktails

elsa petersen-schepelern

photography by james merrell,
william lingwood, and debi treloar

RYLAND
PETERS
& SMALL

London New York

Designer Emilie Ekström
Editor Miriam Hyslop
Production Meryl Silbert
Art Director Gabriella Le Grazie
Publishing Director Alison Starling

Food Stylists Elsa Petersen-Schepelern,
Bridget Sargeson, David Peacock
Stylists Wei Tang, Helen Trent

First published in the United States in 2002
by Ryland Peters & Small, Inc.
519 Broadway, 5th Floor
New York, NY 10012
www.rylandpeters.com

10 9 8 7 6 5 4 3 2 1

Printed in China

Library of Congress Cataloging-in-Publication Data

Petersen-Schepelern, Elsa.

  Cool smoothies : juices and cocktails / Elsa
Petersen-Schepelern.

    p.cm.

  ISBN 1-84172-280-4

  1. Fruit drinks. 2. Smoothies (Beverages) I. Title.

TX815.P45 2002

  641.8'75—dc21   20001048753

Author's Acknowledgments
My heartfelt thanks to James Merrell, William
Lingwood, and Debi Treloar for their beautiful
photographs, to Wei Tang and Helen Trent for
delightful props, and to two of my favorite designers,
Emilie Ekström and Louise Leffler, for making me
look good. Thanks also to my family, Kirsten Bray,
Peter Bray, and Nowelle Valentino-Capezza, and to
friends who helped imbibe these goodies, Tim,
Tessa, Martin, Susan, Sheridan, Mike, and Karen.

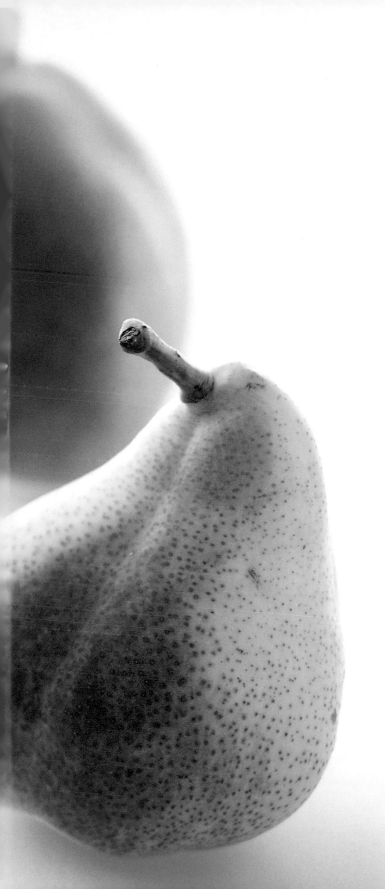

contents

a cool smooth summer

Drinks in the garden, lunch on the deck, barbecues, tennis parties, and sunbathing—all essential summer pastimes requiring the drinks in this book. You'll find recipes for children and adults, drinks with and without alcohol, cocktails for one, or party drinks for many. Almost all include fruit and vegetables and are an easy, delicious way to imbibe your vitamins.

fruits of the earth

Fruit smoothies, juices, and shakes—what better ways can there be to have the five daily servings of fruit and vegetables that doctors recommend for good health? All you need is a blender—a hand-held stick blender will do— or a juicing machine if you're very lucky, and this healthy, delicious collection of fruit drinks is within your grasp.

strawberry
ice cream
smoothie

Strawberry smoothies are invariably the most popular with guests—and with me! Serve them made just with ice, or with yogurt (to make a lassi), ice cream, or milk. Or with the lot. Self-indulgence is a very good thing, in my view.

A variation on this recipe doesn't even need a blender—make a Strawberry Spider in a tall glass with a scoop of strawberry ice cream, 1 tablespoon liqueur or strawberry syrup, then top up with soda (preferably strawberry). Pour in the soda very carefully: it fizzes like mad!

12 ice cubes
4 scoops strawberry ice cream
12 large, ripe strawberries, hulled and halved
½ cup plain low-fat yogurt, or to taste
low-fat milk, to taste
SERVES 1–2

Put the ice cubes into a blender and blend to a snow. Add the ice cream, strawberries, and yogurt and blend again, adding just enough milk to let the blades run. Pour into glasses and serve.

VARIATION Add extra ice cream for a thicker smoothie, or extra milk, to taste. Serve with an extra small scoop of ice cream balanced on the edge of the glass (if possible).

fruit salad lassi
with
strawberries

Lassi is the famous Indian drink made with yogurt and ice, thinned down with a little water. It is served either salty or sweet, flavored with fruit, nuts, or spices. It is very cool and refreshing on a hot summer's day.

Strawberries, mangoes, papayas, or bananas are perfect fruits to team up with milk and yogurt.

Yogurt is a great source of calcium, especially for women—use the low-fat kind if you're watching your waistline.

1 cup low-fat plain yogurt
½ cup low-fat milk
6 large strawberries, hulled and halved
a choice of other fruit, such as 1 small basket
*   raspberries, 6 apricots, or 2 peaches, pitted*
sugar, to taste
crushed ice, to serve
SERVES 2–4

Put the yogurt, milk, strawberries, and other fruit into a blender and process until creamy. Add sugar to taste and serve poured over crushed ice.

VARIATION Instead of the fruit listed, use the pulp and seeds of 4 passionfruit, plus 1 tablespoon Galliano or Grand Marnier liqueur.

strawberry juice
with balsamic

Balsamic—the rich, slightly sweet, aged vinegar from Italy—should be used in moderation: use it like a spice, don't slap it on like ordinary vinegar. It also has an extraordinary affinity with strawberries. Rinse the berries before hulling, or they will fill with water.

2 baskets ripe strawberries

1 tablespoon honey (optional)

6 ice cubes

balsamic vinegar

SERVES 2–4

Reserve a few strawberries for decoration, then put the remainder into a blender with the honey, if using, and the ice cubes. Blend well, adding water if necessary to make the mixture easier to work. Blend again, then serve in a tiny shot glass, over ice, with a halved strawberry on top. Serve the balsamic separately, in drops.

Strawberries with balsamic vinegar—it sounds a rather odd combination, but balsamic acts like lemon juice, to point up other flavors, and its sweet, spicy undertones have an extraordinarily delicious effect. Vinegar also acts as an aid to digestion, prevents fatigue, and lessens the risk of high blood pressure.

pineapple and
strawberry crush

A summer cooler that's simply the most glorious color and tastes like heaven!

1 medium pineapple, peeled and cored
10–12 ripe strawberries
grated zest and juice of 2 lemons
2 tablespoons confectioners' sugar, or to taste
juice of 2 oranges

to serve

ice cubes or crushed ice
3–6 strawberries, sliced
a twist of orange, lime, or lemon zest
SERVES 6–8

Put the pineapple, strawberries, lemon zest, and confectioners' sugar into a blender, add about ½ cup ice water, and purée until smooth. Add the orange and lemon juices and another ½ cup ice water. Taste and add extra sugar if necessary (depending on the sweetness of the fruit). Pour into a pitcher of ice and decorate with sliced berries and a twist of orange or lemon peel.

rhubarb
strawberryade

This unusual, old-fashioned drink is based on homemade lemonade. Make it with pretty pink forced rhubarb for an utterly stunning color, or add a dash of Grenadine to point up the pink.

1 lb. rhubarb, trimmed and sliced
2 tablespoons confectioners' sugar
grated zest and juice of 1 lemon
6 strawberries, hulled and halved

to serve

ice cubes or crushed ice
sparkling water
SERVES 4–8

Put the rhubarb, sugar, and lemon zest into a saucepan and cover with at least 1 quart boiling water. Stew until the rhubarb is very soft. Add the strawberries and boil hard for about 1 minute, then strain into a pitcher, cool, and chill. To serve, pour into a pitcher of ice, stir in the lemon juice, and top up with sparkling water.

Strawberries in any guise please the palate and look wonderfully pretty. They're terrific with pineapple and sensational with rhubarb.

summer fruit crush
with peach,
nectarine, apricots,
and raspberries

In summer, when fruit is good quality, plentiful, and relatively inexpensive, make this fruity mixture in bigger quantities for a party. Take care with your choice of fruit though—keep it red, orange, and yellow —if you add green fruits, such as kiwifruit, you'll spoil the color. Blend the fruit with ice to break up the fibers and help extract all the juice.

I like it made with sparkling water, but you could use cherryade for a children's party. If the fruit is sweet and ripe you may not need any sugar or honey.

1 ripe peach, peeled and halved

1 ripe nectarine, halved

2 ripe apricots, halved

a handful of raspberries

6 ice cubes

sparkling water, to taste

honey or sugar (optional)

SERVES 2

Discard the stones from the fruit. Put the fruit into a blender, then add the ice and enough sparkling water to make the blades run. Blend to a purée.

Add honey or sugar to taste, then enough extra water to produce the consistency you like. Pour into glasses and serve.

Most berries are better blended rather than juiced and are delicious mixed with other fruits. They are also good mixed with yogurt in smoothies and lassis. (In fact, plain low-fat yogurt is the best form of calcium for women and will help soothe your digestion.)

berry ice blocks
with buttermilk
froth

Freeze a selection of fresh juices in an ice cube tray and serve with buttermilk for a delicious breakfast on a hot day. These ice cubes have been made with cranberry juice and strawberry purée.

1 tray of ice cubes made with fruit juices
2 cups buttermilk or low-fat yogurt
sparkling water or club soda (optional)
honey, to taste

SERVES 4

Fill 4 glasses with the fruity ice cubes, add a dollop of buttermilk or yogurt, then top with sparkling water or club soda, if using. Serve honey separately and add to taste.

The ice cubes melt slowly into the drink, so you can top it up with more buttermilk or more sparkling water for a long, cool, delicious and filling drink.

Modern buttermilks are simply skimmed milks blended with a light culture, similar to yogurt. Serve poured over frozen fruit juices. Ice cubes made from fruit juice melt more slowly than ordinary cubes—so they're good for a long, leisurely breakfast (and kids love them too!)

cranberry
cooler

Cranberry mixed with citrus juice is a marriage made in heaven—the prettiest, cloudy pink. The most famous is, of course, the Sea Breeze, but if you're aiming for a healthful drink early in the day, rather than at the cocktail hour, this cooler is for you. Supermarkets sell many versions of cranberry juice, both sweetened and unsweetened. I prefer it unsweetened, but please yourself.

crushed ice
1 cup cranberry juice
1 cup orange juice

to serve
sparkling water
a twist of orange peel
SERVES 1–2

Fill a pitcher with ice, pour over the cranberry and orange juice, and stir well. Top up with sparkling water and serve with a twist of orange peel.

Whole cranberries are usually cooked, because they are very tart indeed. The juice is available sweetened or unsweetened, so choose one to suit your taste. Cranberries are high in vitamin C and antioxidants, which protect against cancer and heart disease, and help ease the pain of arthritis.

A daily helping of blueberries contains enough antioxidants to improve balance, coordination, and short-term memory.

red berry
smoothie

Even people with dairy intolerance are often able to eat yogurt, since it changes its structure during fermentation. It's marvelous for upset stomachs too!

*1 basket berries, about 8 oz., such as
    strawberries, cranberries, red currants, or
    raspberries (for a pink smoothie) or blackberries
    and blueberries (for a blue smoothie)*
1 cup plain yogurt
½ cup crushed ice
sugar or honey, to taste
SERVES 2–3

Put all the ingredients into a blender and work to a thin, frothy cream. If too thick, add water to create a pourable consistency.

Taste, then add sugar or honey if you prefer.

Vitamin C is vital for life and fresh fruit and juice is the best way of getting it. Commercial juices are often pasteurized or heat-treated to sterilize and preserve them. Heat destroys vitamin C, so manufacturers replace it in the form of ascorbic acid. Remember, real fruit contains real vitamins.

blueberry and
orange smoothie

freshly squeezed juice of 4 oranges
1 basket blueberries, about 8 oz.
sugar (optional)

SERVES 1–2

Put the orange juice into a blender, add the blueberries and blend until smooth. Add sugar to taste, if using.

Alternatively, I often peel the oranges, then feed half of them through a juicer, followed by the blueberries, then the remaining oranges.

berry, apricot, and
orange slush

Orange juice will help to extend more expensive fruits, and their gentle acidity also develops the flavor. Apricots are very dense, so you may like to pulp them in the blender rather than putting them through the juicer. If you do decide to juice, remove the skins first, and juice them alternately with pieces of apple.

8 ripe apricots, halved and pitted,
  then coarsely chopped
8 strawberries, hulled and halved
juice of 2 oranges
SERVES 1

Put the apricots, strawberries, and orange juice into a blender and purée until smooth, adding water if needed. (If the mixture is too thick, add a few ice cubes and blend again.)

Note To remove the apricot skins, bring a saucepan of water to a boil, then blanch the apricots for about 1 minute. Remove the skin with the back of a knife.

granny's orangeade

My grandmother was rather good at cooking—a talent she passed on to my mother. I found this deliciously orangy recipe scribbled in one of her falling-apart, yellowing cookbooks.

4 oranges
1 tablespoon sugar, or to taste
freshly squeezed juice of 1 lemon
ice, to serve
SERVES 2–4

Peel the zest from the oranges, leaving the white pith behind. Put the zest into a pitcher with the sugar, then add the orange and lemon juice. Pour over 1 quart boiling water, let stand until cool, strain, and serve over ice.

All fruits contain vitamin C, but oranges remain the benchmark against which all others are measured. Use them to extend fruits that don't have much juice themselves, such as blueberries, strawberries, or apricots.

old-fashioned orangeade

These old-fashioned drinks are not fizzy like modern soft drinks. For fizz, make a stronger mixture by decreasing the quantity of water, then serve the drinks topped up with sparkling water or soda. I added fizz by serving through a Sodastream® machine.

2 oranges, sliced and seeded, but unpeeled
1 lemon, sliced and seeded, but unpeeled
¼ cup sugar, or to taste
a curl of orange zest, to serve
ice, to serve
SERVES 2–4

Put the sliced oranges, lemon, and sugar into a large pitcher, pour over 4–5 cups boiling water, cover, cool, and chill. Serve, strained over glasses of ice, with a curl of orange zest.

Alternatively, double the quantity of fruit, peel the zest, discarding any white pith. Put the zest into a pitcher, add 2 tablespoons sugar, then the citrus juices. Fill with boiling water and let stand until cool. Taste and stir in extra sugar if necessary. Strain into a pitcher of ice and serve in tall glasses.

VARIATIONS *TANGERINEADE OR LIMEADE*
Other citrus fruits can be made into lemonade-style drinks. Grate the zest of 6 tangerines or mandarins or 10 limes, leaving the white pith behind. Put the zest into a pitcher with a little sugar, then add the juice of all the fruit. Pour over 1 quart boiling water, let stand until cool, strain, and serve over ice. You can also use less water and add club soda or sparkling water to serve.

lemon barley water

This soothing, cooling, old-fashioned drink is incredibly easy to make since the invention of the French press—the coffee maker with the plunger. In Victorian times, platoons of kitchen maids would boil up the lemon and barley, strain it through cheesecloth into enormous pitchers, leave it to cool, then try to chill it with whatever technology was available in the Big House at the time. Lucky us— we have the French press and ice. So much easier! The Apple Water variation is wonderful.

2 tablespoons pearl barley

grated zest and juice of 1 large, unwaxed lemon

2 teaspoons sugar

a curl of lemon peel

ice, to serve

SERVES 2 4

Put the barley into a saucepan, add 6 cups boiling water, and simmer for 30 minutes. Strain into a French press, then stir in the sugar, lemon zest, and juice. Cool, plunge, chill, then serve over ice, decorated with a curl of lemon peel.

VARIATION APPLE WATER

Put the juice and zest of ½ lemon, 3 cored, sliced apples, and 1 tablespoon sugar into a food processor and work to a purée. Transfer to a French press and pour over 3 cups boiling water. Cool, plunge, and chill before serving.

real lemonade

We've all had commercial lemonade, which is little more than fizzy sugar water. Real lemonade, on the other hand, is cool and refreshing and actually tastes of lemons. This recipe is a good old-fashioned lemonade, adapted from hand-written recipe books lent by aunts and grandmothers. It always reminds me of tennis parties, wicker chairs on the lawn, drinks in the cool shade of the verandah—and lemonade served by my mother, the last woman in the world to use a parasol!

¼ cup sugar

1½ tablespoons lemon juice

a pinch of salt

mint leaves

a few slices of lemon

ice, to serve

SERVES 4–8

Put the sugar and ½ cup water into a saucepan and boil for 2 minutes. Chill, then stir in the lemon juice and salt. Transfer to a large glass pitcher and add about 4 cups water. Add the mint leaves and lemon slices. Fill with ice, stir, and serve.

Lemon juice is good for the digestion. Its sharp taste can also be used instead of salt to enhance other flavors.

ice lime tea

1 quart freshly made tea, lightly brewed
sugar, to taste
1–2 unwaxed limes, finely sliced
ice cubes
sparkling water, lemonade, or ginger ale
SERVES 4

Strain the tea into a pitcher, stir in the sugar, cool, and chill. Put sliced limes into a serving pitcher, then half-fill it with ice cubes. Half-fill the pitcher with the cold tea, then top up with sparkling water, lemonade, or ginger ale, stir, and serve.

hot lemon tea

1 unwaxed lemon
1 tablespoon honey
1 pot of tea
SERVES 1

Cut 2 slices off the lemon and squeeze the juice from the rest. Put the honey and sliced lemon into a large mug, add the lemon juice, then top with tea. Stir and drink.

fresh lime soda

I have been to India many times, and it never seems to get any cooler!

My favorite thirst-quencher—served everywhere from five-star hotels to village truck-stops—is this fresh lime soda, served either with salt or sugar (or, in my case, plain).

Indian limes are inclined to be yellow, rather than green, and half the size of ordinary limes. They seem to be extra-juicy and not as tart as the green ones.

You wouldn't think that salty drinks could be at all pleasant, but Indians serve fresh lime sodas and yogurt lassi drinks with a pinch of salt, and they are incredibly cooling. Try it and see!

freshly squeezed juice of 1–2 limes
1 small bottle club soda or sparkling water
sugar or sea salt, to taste
crushed ice or ice cubes (optional)
SERVES 1

Put the lime juice into a tall glass. Serve with a bottle of club soda or sparkling water, and small dishes of salt or sugar, according to taste. Crushed ice or ice cubes may also be added.

citron pressé

Surprisingly, the French version, the Citron Pressé, is very similar to Fresh Lime Soda. Lemon juice is squeezed into a glass, then served with a separate pitcher of ice water and a bowl of sugar. I think this is just the perfect cooler in the middle of a hard day's shopping in Paris!

1 lemon, squeezed

to serve
a small pitcher of ice water
sugar
SERVES 1

Put the lemon juice into a tall glass and put onto a small plate with a small napkin under the glass. Serve with a pitcher of ice water, a small dish of sugar, and a long spoon.

Lemons and limes are high in vitamin C and become sweeter and juicier as they ripen. They have an antibacterial and decongestant action, so are excellent for coughs and colds.

banana and honey breakfast smoothie

A filling breakfast—full of flavor, packed with calcium and fiber, and very good for you! If you like your drinks less sweet, reduce the quantity of honey. You can also substitute other fruit in season, such as berries. Use chilled fruit to make smoothies, but never keep bananas in the refrigerator—or anywhere near citrus fruit—they don't like it. They quickly turn black in the refrigerator, and become over-ripe in a flash if introduced to a citrus fruit.

1 cup low-fat milk

1 cup low-fat yogurt

2 tablespoons crushed ice

1 tablespoon honey

1 banana

1 tablespoon wheatgerm

SERVES 2–4

Put all the ingredients into a blender and blend until smooth. Add extra fruit if preferred.

banana and papaya
smoothie

Bananas and papayas won't juice effectively—their pulp is too dense—but they are definitely candidates for the blender treatment. If your blender doesn't crush ice, add it at the end, but, to help the machine run, you will need a little water, yogurt, or juice.

1 small papaya, peeled, seeded, and
  cut into chunks
1 banana, peeled and cut into chunks
about 6 ice cubes
1 tablespoon wheatgerm (optional)
½ cup yogurt or water (optional)
SERVES 2–4

Put the papaya and banana into a blender with the ice and ½ cup water or yogurt, if using. Blend until smooth, then add the wheatgerm, if using, and extra water or yogurt to form a pourable consistency, then serve.

VARIATION Blueberries and banana make a famous combination. Blend them with ice, yogurt, and a dash of honey.

Bananas are high in complex carbohydrates—
that's why you see tennis players eating
them at Wimbledon. Very nourishing and
good for your cholesterol levels.

banana
and coconut shake

Coconut milk and bananas are a traditional Thai combination—I've added dark rum as an optional extra. The result is a Thailand-meets-the-Caribbean mix!

about 1 cup canned coconut milk

1 cup low-fat milk

2 ripe bananas, cut into chunks

1 tablespoon dark rum, or to taste (optional)

sugar, to taste

crushed ice, to serve

SERVES 1–2

Put the coconut milk into a blender, then add the milk, bananas, and rum, if using. Blend until smooth, then add sugar to taste (and extra rum if you like). Blend again, then pour over crushed ice and serve.

bananas
and limes with ginger ale

Bananas and limes are typical Southeast Asian ingredients, as is ginger, though not usually in this form. Lychees, if you can find them, make a delicious substitute for the bananas—they are sold either fresh or canned in Asian markets.

2–3 large bananas, cut into chunks

grated zest and juice of 2 limes

ginger ale, to taste

sugar, to taste

crushed ice, to serve

SERVES 2

Put the bananas into a blender, then add the lime zest and juice and a little ginger ale. Blend well, then and add sugar to taste. Half-fill the glasses with crushed ice, pour over the mixture, and top up with more ginger ale.

Bananas are energy foods—rich in potassium, vitamins A, C, and K. They can be meal in themselves—wonderful for breakfast and good for growing

pineapple
and lime crush

To keep cut pineapple in the refrigerator, wrap it in plastic wrap to prevent it tainting other foods. Fruit varies in sweetness, so taste the crush before serving and add sugar to taste. This drink is also great made with ice cream instead of the yogurt or coconut milk, though you will have to add a little chilled milk, or the drink will be too thick.

1¼ cups yogurt or coconut milk
8 oz. chopped fresh ripe pineapple*
juice and grated rind of 2 limes
1 cup crushed ice
sugar, to taste
finely sliced fresh coconut (optional)
1 scoop vanilla ice cream (optional)
SERVES 1–2

Put the first 4 ingredients into a blender and purée until smooth. Add sugar to taste and serve topped with fresh coconut or ice cream, if using.

*Note If you haven't done it before, peeling a pineapple can be tricky. Put the pineapple on its side with the prickly top hanging over the edge of the bench. Grasp it firmly and jerk it down—the top will come off. Discard it. Cut off both ends to make them flat, then put the pineapple on the flat bottom. Slice the skin off vertically, cut out the prickly "eyes" with the tip of a sharp knife, then cut into wedges and cut out and discard the cores.

banana, honey,
and soy milk smoothie

A good breakfast smoothie—and full of protein from the soy milk. It is quite sweet, so taste the mixture before adding any extra honey. Other fruits, such as strawberries, or papaya, can be used instead of the banana.

1 banana, cut into chunks
1 teaspoon honey
1 cup soy milk
1 cup crushed ice (optional)
sprigs of mint, to serve (optional)
SERVES 1

Put the banana, honey, and soy milk into a blender with the crushed ice, if using, and blend until smooth. Serve, topped with sprigs of mint.

pineapple crush

1 large pineapple

1 lemon

ice cubes

4 passionfruit (optional)

sugar or honey, to taste

SERVES 4

Peel the pineapple as on the previous page. Cut it into wedges, then chunks, then press through a juicer. Add the juice of 1 lemon and pour the mixture into a pitcher of ice. Stir in the flesh and seeds of 3 passionfruit, if using, and top with the remaining flesh and seeds. Depending on the sweetness and ripeness of the pineapple, you may like to add a little sugar or honey.

Fresh pineapple contains the enzyme bromelian, which helps with digestion. It is soothing for sore throats, coughs, and upset stomachs.

Eating ripe fresh mangoes is good for your skin and for high blood pressure. Mangoes are better blended rather than juiced and are good mixed with other ingredients, such as coconut milk or yogurt.

mango
ginger lassi

This mango lassi is made with the Indian Alphonso—the world's greatest mango. If you can't find him fresh, purée any variety of sweet mango in a blender. The good-quality canned Alphonso mango purée sold by Asian grocers can also be used instead (and tastes spectacular).

1 cup mango purée*
1 cup low-fat plain yogurt
1 tablespoon ginger purée (pages 49, 79)
crushed ice
1 quart ginger beer
SERVES 6–8 OR MORE

Put the first 4 ingredients into a pitcher and mix well (I use a pair of chopsticks). Top up with ginger beer and serve.

*Note You can also use frozen mango—just put 8 oz. into a blender with a few tablespoons of water and blend until smooth.

mango and
coconut milk

A nut-milk recipe that's particularly good for people who are lactose-intolerant—and for anyone lucky enough to have too many mangoes.

2 fresh ripe mangoes, peeled and pitted, frozen
  mango, or 1 cup mango purée (page 44)
juice of ½ lime or lemon
1 cup unsweetened shredded dried coconut
  (measured by volume), or canned coconut milk

SERVES 2

Blend the mangoes with the lime or lemon juice, then transfer to a pitcher and chill.

If using dried coconut, put it into a blender with 1 cup ice water. Blend until frothy, let stand for 5 minutes, then blend again. Strain into the pitcher and return the coconut to the blender. Repeat with another 1 cup ice water. Strain, then stir into the pitcher of mango and lime or lemon. Serve immediately. Alternatively, omit the coconut milk and just blend the mango and lime or lemon juice with enough ice cubes and water to make a pourable consistency.

When properly ripe, mango skin can be removed a little like a banana skin. If you have to peel it with a knife, it's not ripe enough.

watermelon
and ginger sharbat

Indian and Moroccan sharbats are distantly related to the sherbets which are familiar to Westerners. They were introduced to India by the Moghul emperors who invaded over its Northwest Frontier in the 16th century.

If you have a juicer, use it to make watermelon juice—though, I must admit, I sometimes prefer the thicker consistency produced by a food processor. You can buy ginger purée in supermarkets, but, if you can't find it, just peel and slice fresh ginger and purée in a food processor with a little water or lemon juice, then freeze in ice cube trays for future use.

1 small, ripe watermelon, chilled
2 tablespoons ginger purée, or to taste
sugar, to taste
crushed ice, to serve
SERVES 2–4

Cut the watermelon in half, then remove and discard the rind and seeds. Put the watermelon flesh and ginger into a food processor and blend until smooth. Add water if the mixture is too thick. Taste and add sugar if needed, then serve over crushed ice.

watermelon
and lime slush

Turn your sharbat into a slush, a frappé, or a granita, and point up the flavor with a little lime juice.

1 small, ripe watermelon, chilled
2 inches fresh ginger, peeled and grated
crushed ice
2 limes, cut into wedges
SERVES 4

Prepare the watermelon and ginger as in the previous recipe and put the flesh through a juicer. Serve in glasses half-filled with crushed ice and top with wedges of lime for squeezing.

To make a frappé or granita, add sugar to taste (the mixture should be very sweet), then freeze in small, shallow containers. Just before serving, crush into icy shards and serve as a granita at the end of a meal. Alternatively, crush into an icy slush and serve as a frappé drink.

Many fruit juices can be frozen, then crushed with a fork to form a granita to serve in a bowl, or crushed further to form a frappé, served as a drink.

melon froth

The four melon varieties used in this drink are my favorites and all very aromatic. My juicer produces a froth, but if yours is less muscular, you could layer the juices to form orange and green stripes. Wonderful for a summer brunch party.

1–2 melons—orange cantaloupe or charentais, or green galia or honeydew, halved, seeded, and peeled

ginger syrup, to taste (optional)

SERVES 1–2

Put the melons through a juicer. Layer the colors in glasses if preferred, or serve separately. If using ginger syrup, serve it separately.

Melons have a delicate, elusive flavor and a delightful texture. Melon and ginger is one of the great food marriages, so a dash of ground ginger or fresh ginger juice is utterly wonderful.

apple
lemonade

This recipe is best made with cooking apples—they turn to delicious apple-flavored foam when boiled.

For a much quicker result, use fresh apple juice, omit the sugar, add the fresh lemon juice, and fill with mineral water.

2–3 cooking apples, unpeeled,
 chopped into small pieces
sugar, to taste
juice of 1 lemon

to serve
sparkling water
ice
SERVES 4

Put the apples into a saucepan, cover with cold water, bring to a boil, and simmer until soft. Strain, pressing the pulp through the strainer with a spoon. Add sugar to taste, stir until dissolved, then let cool.

To serve, pack a pitcher with ice, half-fill the glass with the apple juice, add the lemon juice, and top with sparkling water.

Cooked apple drinks are usually pale, but fresh juices made from red apples will be pink if you juice them with the skins on.

apple juice
with fennel

Fennel can be very difficult to juice—
you need a strong machine. Alternatively,
chop it and purée in a blender with apple
juice, then strain. Use a crisp, sweet,
red apple such as Red Delicious to give
a wonderful pinkish tinge. Always
remember to remove the stem and stalk
ends of apples and pears, where any
pesticides and residues collect.

1 fennel bulb, including sprigs of the
   feathery leaves
2 apples, cored but not peeled
juice of ½ lemon (optional)

SERVES 1–2

Trim the green leaves from the fennel bulb, trim off
the root end, then slice the bulb into long wedges
and cut out and remove the cores from each
wedge. Cut the apple into wedges. Put the apples
and fennel through a juicer.

Stir in the lemon juice to stop discoloration, then
serve immediately, topped with a few fennel sprigs
for extra scent.

minty
ginger
granny smith

Any apples will do, but unpeeled Granny Smiths produce the most beautiful green. The ginger is optional, but utterly delicious, and the mint leaves give an even brighter green. Just a hint—we professional dieters know to use apple juice instead of sugar to add sweetness. Lime juice will stop the apple juice turning brown so quickly, but drink this concoction immediately—don't let it hang around, or you lose all the benefits of freshly crushed juice.

*4 Granny Smith apples, cored but not peeled, then
    cut into chunks
a chunk of fresh ginger, peeled and sliced
4–8 sprigs of mint
1 tablespoon fresh lime juice (optional)*
SERVES 1

Push half the apples through a juicer, then the ginger, mint, and lime juice, if using. Finally, push through the remaining apples and serve.

VARIATION *FROZEN APPLE MARGARITA*
Put 1 cup crushed ice into a blender, add the juice, and blend to a froth. The Margarita is ready when the sound of the motor changes—that means the mixture has risen away from the blades.

Apples are particularly good for the heart and blood and can help to lower cholesterol levels.

vegetable magic

Most vegetables are better for you uncooked, because cooking destroys many vitamins, such as vitamin C. Salads and crudités are good ways to serve them, but juicing is probably the quickest and easiest way of all. There are many inexpensive juicers on the market now: I keep mine out on the bench and use it every day to make fruit and vegetable juices. Perfect for breakfast!

Carrots are high in beta carotene, which the body uses to convert into vitamin A.

carrot and
ginger crush

Carrot juice, so naturally sweet, is my absolutely favorite juice. Though carrots are better for you when cooked, I much prefer them raw. Just make sure you peel them first, unless they have been organically grown.

5 medium carrots, peeled
a chunk of fresh ginger, peeled and sliced
   (optional)
SERVES 1–2

Cut the carrots into pieces small enough to fit through the feeder tube. When half the carrots have been processed, add the ginger, if using, then the rest of the carrots.

Note Don't drink carrot juice more than 2–3 times a week, or your skin may develop an orange, carroty tinge!

tomato, celery, and **carrot** crush

Juicers are wonderful machines. Fresh foaming carrot juice is my favorite, but try this spicy combination too. You could substitute 2 seeded chiles instead of the Tabasco sauce, for a fresh, bright chile taste. Chill all the vegetables first, for a summer cooler.

2 lb. carrots

3 celery stalks

1 lb. tomatoes

salt and freshly ground black pepper

Tabasco sauce, to taste

crushed ice, to serve

SERVES 4–6

Push the carrots, celery, and tomatoes through a juicer. Alternatively, purée in a food processor with 1 cup ice water, then press through a strainer. Add salt, pepper, and Tabasco, to taste. Serve poured over crushed ice.

The tomato is one of the healthiest of all vegetables—what better excuse to have a Bloody Mary? Mixed with carrots and celery, it's a real vitamin powerhouse.

celery and grapes

Celery juice is marvelous when mixed with other vegetable juices—and also with juicy fruits such as grapes. You can buy grape juice, but fresh juice is a revelation. White grapes will produce a fresh green juice—red ones give a delicious pink-tinged nectar.

6 celery stalks, trimmed

about 20 seedless white grapes

1 bunch watercress (optional)

ice cubes

SERVES 1–2

Push the celery stalks into the juicer, leaf end first. Alternate with the grapes, which are very soft and difficult to push through on their own. Press through the watercress, if using, and serve plain, in glasses filled with ice, or put into a blender with ice cubes to produce a delicious celery-grape froth.

Celery has almost no calories—it's like eating water, so is marvelous for dieters. Celery is also a natural tranquilizer, so sip and snooze.

Peppers and their hot-headed chile cousins have three times as much vitamin C as an orange. Juicing removes the indigestible skins and extracts all the sweet flavor.

mexican golden salsa crush

Peppers, tomatoes, and chiles originally came from Mexico. I am not very fond of fiery-hot chiles, so one medium-hot one is plenty for me. Add more if you like, or use a hotter one. the pinch of salt is optional, but salt will point up the flavor beautifully. If you're a proponent of the salt-free diet, try a dash of freshly squeezed lemon juice instead.

2 red, orange, or yellow bell peppers,
  halved and seeded
1 medium-hot red chile, seeded
2 tomatoes, quartered
a pinch of salt or a squeeze of lemon juice
  (optional)
ice, to serve (optional)

SERVES 1

Push 1 bell pepper through the juicer, then the chile, tomatoes, and salt or lemon juice, if using. Push through the remaining bell pepper and serve immediately, over ice, if using.

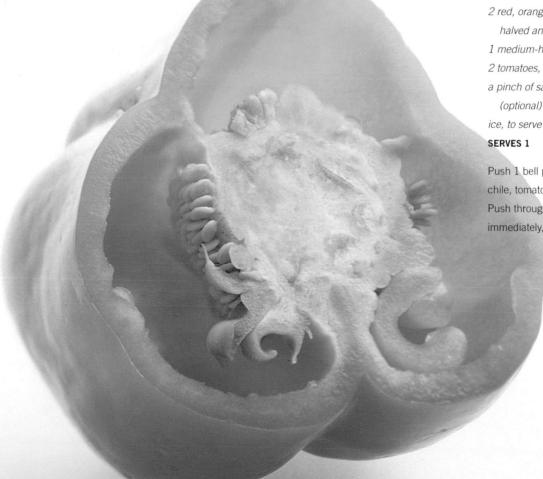

beet
and orange juice

Raw beets are good for you, but only in small quantities—and they have a decidedly earthy taste. Trimming and peeling before juicing will help, but I like to "stretch" them with freshly squeezed juice such as orange or apple. Depending on the sweetness of the oranges, you may need a little honey as well.

1 medium beet, trimmed and peeled
2–3 oranges
honey, to taste
SERVES 1

Cut the beet into pieces and press through a juicer. Squeeze the oranges. Mix and taste, adding honey if necessary.

Note Beet leaves are also delicious—juice them separately or with spinach leaves. Alternatively, sauté in a little olive oil and serve as an accompaniment to entrées.

Beets, famous as a blood tonic, are a powerhouse of vitamins and minerals. They are good for blood pressure, protect against anaemia, and promote general good health.

lettuce and
parsley crush

Lettuce and parsley produce small quantities of juice and taste decidedly green! So add the juice of an apple or other fruit as an extender and sweetener. As many good cooks know, much of the flavor in parsley is in the stalks, so juice them too. Before juicing, all leafy vegetables should be washed well, wrapped in a cloth, and chilled until crisp.

1 romaine or iceberg lettuce, stalk trimmed

1 large bunch of parsley, including stalks,
  ends trimmed

1 green apple, cored and quartered,
  but not peeled

SERVES 1

Form the lettuce and parsley leaves into balls and push through the feed tube of the juicer. Push the apple through (this will extract more juice from the lettuce and parsley). Stir if necessary, then serve immediately—don't wait.

Parsley is famous as a breath freshener and an effective digestive. Lettuce is high in antioxidants—and iceberg is a particularly juicy variety. Cucumber is low in calories but rich in vitamins B1, B2, and C, and the minerals calcium and iron.

cucumber juice
with spinach

Spinach is high in iron, but not in a form easily used by the body. In fact, too much isn't good for you. It got its "ironic" reputation because, when the original testing was done in the 1800s, someone got the decimal point in the wrong place and the mistake wasn't discovered until it was retested in 1947. Drinking spinach juice is no-one's idea of a good time, but if you mix it with something more delicious you'll absorb all its goodness almost painlessly. Apple or cucumber are both good choices. If using cucumbers, try to use organically grown produce. Others are often waxed and must be peeled first (so you lose some of the color and nutrients).

1 organic cucumber, about 12 inches long,
   quartered lengthwise
1 large handful of well-washed spinach
salt or lemon juice, to taste (optional)
SERVES 1–2

Juice half the cucumber, then all the spinach, then the remaining cucumber. Add salt or lemon juice to taste, if using.

VARIATION Cucumber has a cooling, astringent effect—to sweeten it, use half-and-half with apple juice from crisp Granny Smiths.

herbs, spices, and nuts

Herbs and spices can add extra pizzazz to smoothies and fruit juices—and they're utterly gorgeous used to add flavor to tea, or to make an infusion. Many have healthful properties as well as tasting great. Nuts, ground with milk or water to make nut milk, were used as invalid food in olden times—these days, most cooks use them just for their flavor and their creamy, delicious smoothness.

rosemary tisane

Tisane is a French word which means an infusion of herbs, flowers, or leaves, usually dried—a kind of tea, in other words. I prefer tisanes made with fresh ingredients where possible. In early times, they were seen as cures for many ailments. Nowadays, people drink them because they taste good. A *tisanière* is a tall, lidded cup, with a strainer inside to hold the herb. If you don't have one (they can sometimes be found in antique shops), use a French press instead.

4–6 sprigs of rosemary

1–2 teaspoons honey

SERVES 1–2

Put the rosemary and honey into a French press or teapot, cover with boiling water, let infuse for about 5 minutes, then plunge or strain.

VARIATIONS Tisanes can also be made with camomile flowers, lemon balm, marjoram, sage, thyme, and orange blossoms.

Rosemary tea will wake you up, so drink it only in the morning (it's also good for a hangover). Lavender is mildly sedative, so it's good to drink before bed or when you need to relax.

lavender tea

The very essence of a hot summer afternoon in Italy or the South of France, lavender tea is wonderfully calming for frazzled nerves: drink it after a hard day at the office, or sip a cup before bed.

1–2 large sprigs of lavender leaves
a few lavender flowers, if available
1 teaspoon honey, or to taste
SERVES 1

Put the lavender into a teapot or one-cup French press and and cover with boiling water. Let steep for about 5 minutes, covered. Put 1 teaspoon honey, if using, into your cup, then press the plunger and pour the tea.

Alternatively, pour the honey over the lavender in the French press before adding the boiling water.

1 large bunch of fresh mint
2 tablespoons leaf tea, such as
Earl Grey or green tea

to serve
mint sprigs
sugar
SERVES 4–6

Fill a French press with mint, add the tea, and pour over boiling water. Let brew for 1–2 minutes (no longer or the tannin will be released from the tea). Push the plunger. To serve hot, pour into small tea glasses with a dish of sugar served separately.

Alternatively, pour the tea into a pitcher. Chill until very cold, then serve in tea glasses with mint and the dish of sugar.

moroccan iced mint tea

Moroccan mint tea is served hot in tiny engraved and gilded glasses—it's the perfect finish to a spicy Moroccan meal and helps oil the wheels of conversation in countless tea shops across the land. I like it hot in the traditional way, but it's also marvelous chilled and iced as a cool summer drink.

I prefer to make it in a French press, then you don't have to bother with straining or fishing out the leaves. If you don't have a French press, you can also make it in a big teapot or pitcher, then strain into a second pitcher before chilling and serving.

Endless glasses of this aromatic brew drive animated conversations in the tea houses of Morocco. Like tea, mint is a stimulant, so don't drink it late at night. However, like ginger, it will help digestion and relieve an upset stomach.

mint tisane

a large bunch of mint

sugar or honey, to taste (optional)

SERVES 1–4

Wash the mint well, then break it into large handfuls and put into a French press. Pour over boiling water, let steep for 3–5 minutes, then press the plunger. Pour into tea glasses, add sugar or honey, if using, and a few mint leaves, then serve.

mint and
ginger
yogurt soda

Mint and ginger make a delicious combination. Ginger purée is sold in some supermarkets—or make it yourself with fresh root ginger in a blender. Plain yogurt has a wonderful lemony taste. I prefer this drink without sugar—so taste it first and decide for yourself.

2 cups plain or low-fat yogurt

leaves from 4 sprigs of mint

1 inch fresh ginger, grated, or

   1 tablespoon ginger purée

2 cups sparkling water, or to taste

sugar, to taste

crushed ice, to serve

SERVES 2–4

Put the yogurt, mint, and ginger into a blender, add about ½ cup sparkling water and blend to a froth. Add sugar to taste. Spoon crushed ice into each glass, pour over the mixture, then top up with more sparkling water.

pineapple
with jamaican
ginger beer

Ginger beer is a favorite drink in Jamaica. Put it together with fresh pineapple and you have an utterly delicious thirst-quencher—the taste of the Caribbean through a straw! Try it mixed with other fresh fruit too, such as very ripe peaches, papayas, or apricots.

3 slices ripe fresh pineapple, chilled

about 1 cup ginger beer, chilled

about 1 cup crushed ice

SERVES 1–2

Put the pineapple into a blender, add about 2–3 tablespoons of the ginger beer, then the crushed ice. Blend well, then pour into tall glasses or mugs and top up with the remaining ginger beer.

ginger tea

a chunk of fresh ginger
1 teaspoon leaf tea (optional)
sweetener of your choice

SERVES 1

Peel and grate the ginger. (The cheese-grater shown here is quick, clean, and easy.) Put into a tea strainer or tea ball, put into a cup, then add the tea, if using. Add boiling water and let steep for 1–5 minutes, according to how strong you like the flavor. Add sweetener if you like, then sip slowly. The same ginger can be used for extra cups.

VARIATION If you're short of time, you don't even need to grate the ginger—just slice it into a cup, then add boiling water.

jamaican
iced ginger
sorrel tea

Jamaican sorrel is the flower of a native hibiscus, sold fresh or dried in Caribbean stores or in health food shops, where it is sometimes labeled as "red hibiscus tea." In Australia and New Zealand, it's known as "rosella" and is used to make jam. It's an unusual, sophisticated taste—not unlike cranberry juice—and, if you like vaguely bitter flavors, you'll love it!

Of course most things Caribbean will go with a swing if you add a good measure of rum. My favorite is a gorgeous golden rum called Mount Gay, but there are others. I prefer golden or dark because they seem to have more flavor than white rum.

1 inch fresh ginger, peeled and sliced or grated
¼ cup dried sorrel flowers or hibiscus tea
¼ cup sugar

to serve
ice
a twist of lime

SERVES 4–8

Put the ginger, sorrel, and sugar into a French press. Pour over boiling water. When the liquid is a light purple (this happens fast!) push the plunger, then serve immediately, or cool and chill. Serve over ice with a twist of lime.

To serve as a longer drink, top up with ginger ale, soda or mineral water. The cocktail below usually has lots of sugar, but I prefer it less sweet.

VARIATION *SORREL RUM COCKTAIL*
Put ¼ cup dried sorrel, a twist of orange peel, 1 cinnamon stick, 6 cloves and 1–2 cups sugar into a French press. Pour over 1½ quarts boiling water, stir well, then push the plunger. Add 2 extra cloves and a cinnamon stick to the top, cool, and chill. To serve, pour over ice, then add a jigger of rum and a cinnamon stick for swizzling.

Dried red sorrel flowers are sold in Caribbean markets— use by themselves to make tea, or add other Caribbean flavors like ginger and lime.

fresh homemade
ginger beer

Our family made ginger beer when I was a kid—the cupboards in the kitchen and the barn always seemed to be full of bottles, which sometimes exploded spectacularly over a period of weeks, as the ginger beer fermented.

This ginger beer is quicker than the traditional kind and I also think the taste is fresher and brighter. Don't peel the ginger if you're blending it in a food processor—just chop it up coarsely, then pulse until well chopped. The skin will give the beer extra flavor.

4 oz. grated fresh ginger
zest and juice of 2 limes
2 cloves
1 cup sugar (brown gives better color)
club soda or sparkling water, to serve
SERVES 4

Put all the ingredients into a large French press or heatproof pitcher, pour over 1 quart boiling water, and stir until the sugar dissolves.

Cool, plunge or strain, then chill well. To serve, half-fill glasses with the mixture and top with club soda or sparkling water.

Ginger isn't just one of the world's great flavors—delicious in sweet or savory dishes—it is also a healthy wonderfood. It is most famous for its ability to calm an upset stomach and soothe indigestion, coughs, and colds. However, it's also a popular folk remedy to help ease the pain of arthritis.

cardamom

green tea

In India, tea is usually made with milk, but in the far north, which had trading links with China, they sometimes use green tea. I discovered this recipe there: a pot of green tea containing an aromatic treasure—a spoonful of green cardamom pods. Often you find a few pods stuffed down the spout of the teapot, so the boiling tea picks up gorgeous flavors as it passes over the spice. If you need an excuse to drink it, remember that, like ginger, cardamom is also a powerful soothing agent for upset stomachs.

1 teaspoon green tea, plus 1 for the pot
6 green cardamom pods
sugar, to taste
SERVES 2

Rinse the teapot with boiling water, add the tea and cardamom, then fill with boiling water. Let steep for 1–2 minutes only (no longer, or the bitter tannins will be released). Pour the tea and add sugar only if you usually like sweet tea.

Cardamom is the basis of "chai masala," an aromatic blend of spices used to flavor tea all over India. Make up your own mixture, adding ginger, cinnamon, cloves, and other favorites.

star anise tea

If you like aniseed flavors, like licorice or pastis, you'll love this drink. Tea is always best made with leaves, but this recipe can also be made with your favorite brand of tea bag. I like it not too strong and served without milk.

1 tea bag, such as English Breakfast
1 whole star anise
sweetener, to taste
milk (optional)
SERVES 1

Put the tea bag and star anise into a cup, add sweetener if you usually use it, then pour over boiling water. Let steep for your usual amount of time, then remove the tea bag and serve, with milk, if using.

coconut milkshake
with **cloves**

I've used ordinary canned coconut milk in this recipe. However, if you'd like to make your own coconut milk, put about 1 cup unsweetened shredded dried coconut into a bowl and cover with milk or water. Let stand for 20 minutes, then press through a strainer. If you don't want to use coconut milk at all, substitute ordinary milk plus coconut syrup, or any kind of fruit syrup.

½ cup milk

1 cup canned coconut milk

3 scoops ice cream

1 teaspoon ground cloves

sugar, to taste

to serve (optional)

crushed ice

finely sliced fresh coconut

SERVES 1–2

Put the milk, coconut milk, ice cream, and cloves into a blender and blend until frothy. Taste and add sugar if required.

Blend again until the sugar has dissolved. Serve over crushed ice, topped with coconut.

Cloves were originally a medicinal spice, supposed to guard against the plague and, for good measure, also regarded as an aphrodisiac. Christmas oranges studded with cloves were originally a talisman against illness.

almond sharbat

The sharbat is the ancestor of sherbet—cool, thirst-quenching, and perfect for people who don't drink alcohol. They can be made with either nuts or fruits, as in Watermelon Sharbat (page 49).

1 cup blanched almonds
a few drops of almond extract (optional)
1 teaspoon rosewater (optional)
crushed seeds from 8 green cardamom pods
sugar, to taste
SERVES 1–2

Put the almonds into a blender, grind to a meal, then add enough water to make a smooth paste. Add the almond extract and rosewater, if using, then the cardamom seeds, 2 cups cold water, and sugar to taste. Blend, then taste and add more sugar if liked. Pour over crushed ice and serve.

almond milk

You can use unblanched almonds (with their skins still on), but the result is browner and grittier. To blanch your own almonds, put into a bowl, cover with boiling water, leave for 5 minutes, then pop them out of their skins.

1 small package almonds, preferably blanched, about 3–4 oz.
1 tablespoon honey
1 cup ice cubes or crushed ice, to serve
SERVES 1–2

Put the almonds and honey into a blender, then add the ice cubes and 1 cup ice water. Blend to a paste. Gradually add extra ice water until the mixture is smooth. Strain and serve over ice.

Nut milks are wonderful for people who "don't do dairy." You can make them with any nuts, but almonds are easy to find. Almond milk was an old-fashioned invalid food: if you're healthy, it will obviously make you even stronger!

clever cocktails

Fruit and fruit juices, spices—and even vegetables, in the case of a Bloody Mary—can all be turned into gorgeous cocktails and long drinks with mixers. Use the ideas here as a base and let your imagination run wild. Usually, all you need is a blender, but sometimes just a cocktail shaker will do. Choose your favorite fruit, then blend it with ice and liquor or liqueur—or pour over chilled champagne or wine and you have a perfect summer drink.

frozen
margarita

Margaritas are my favorite cocktail. They're great but lethal when made properly and, I've found, sometimes almost totally without alcohol when ordered in a bar (probably a good idea!) The usual way of serving margaritas is to dip the rim of the glasses in salt—this is optional, but I think that a twist of lime is absolutely crucial! Some people also like a dash of sugar, though, in my opinion, this depends on the flavor of the limes.

½ cup freshly squeezed lime juice,
  plus extra for the glass
salt, for the glass
⅓ cup Triple Sec or Cointreau
½ cup tequila
6 ice cubes
1 lime, halved and finely sliced lengthwise,
  to serve
salt for the glass

SERVES 4

Dip the rim of each glass onto a saucer of lime juice, then into a second saucer of salt.

Put the lime juice, Triple Sec or Cointreau, and tequila into a blender with crushed ice. Blend until frothy. The sound of the motor will suddenly change as the froth rises above the blades.

Pour into the chilled, salt-rimmed Margarita glasses and serve with a slice of lime.

strawberry
margarita

1 basket ripe strawberries, about 12
1 cup tequila
1 tablespoon powdered sugar
juice of 1 lime
1 tablespoon strawberry syrup
6 ice cubes

SERVES 6

Put all the ingredients into a blender with crushed ice. Blend and serve as in the previous recipe.

cranberry margarita

2 tablespoons tequila
2 tablespoons Cointreau or Triple Sec
juice of ½ lime
¼ cup cranberry juice
6 ice cubes
sugar, to taste

SERVES 2

Put all the ingredients except the sugar into a blender. Blend well, then add sugar to taste.

watermelon gin

I grew up in the tropics, where there were lots of different watermelon varieties. The round ones with dark green skins and orange-red flesh were called sugar-melons, but the enormous torpedo-shaped watermelons, with striped skins and pinky-red flesh, were our favorites.

The seed-free section in the middle of a melon is the sweetest, so if you're cutting pieces for garnish, use this part.

2 very ripe watermelons, well chilled
2–3 cups gin (or to taste)

to serve
crushed ice
sprigs of mint
watermelon triangles (optional)

SERVES 10–20

Cut the watermelon in half and remove the rind and seeds. Working in batches, put the flesh into a blender or food processor and blend until smooth. If the mixture is too thick, add water.

Pour into a pitcher and stir in the gin. Fill glasses with ice, pour over the Watermelon Gin, and serve topped with a sprig of mint and a melon triangle.

VARIATION *LIME AND WATERMELON VODKA*
Substitute vodka instead of the gin, and stir in the juice of 2 limes.

Note Some people blend the watermelon with the seeds still in it, then strain it before serving. I think this spoils the flavor and appearance, and most of the creamy solids are removed during straining. It's well worth taking the time to remove the seeds.

The summery flavor of ripe watermelon goes wonderfully well with the fresh, clean, lemony taste of gin.

1 basket blueberries, about 1½–2 cups
⅓ cup sugar
1 large bottle gin, 750 ml

to serve (optional)
crushed ice
Indian tonic water
sprigs of mint
SERVES 15–20

Put the blueberries into a large glass bottle or empty bottle of spirits. Add the sugar and gin, then shake well and set aside for at least 2 weeks, or up to 2 months. Shake the bottle from time to time—you will see the marvelous rich color developing as the days go by.

Put a shot of the gin into a blender with 3 tablespoons of crushed ice. Blend, then pour into tall, chilled glasses. Add a sprig of mint and tonic to taste.

Alternatively, serve alone in small shot glasses. Do not drive!

blueberry gin

A delicious drink based on English sloe gin, which is made in fall, then set aside until Christmas. I think it should be served in small glasses—it tastes wonderful, but is very heady, and can be something of a trap. You can also serve it in long glasses with ice and tonic water. Delicious and the most marvelous color!

One of the great English Christmastime drinks is sloe gin, made with the fruit of the blackthorn, gathered in the hedgerows in fall, after the first frost. If you don't have a hedgerow handy, blueberries make a delicious substitute.

bloody mary

Make Bloody Mary with fresh tomato juice and your friends will love you forever. Fresh tomato juice is thinner and sweeter than the commercial kinds—and more delicious. I make my tomato juice in a blender—tomatoes are hard to push through a juicer because they are so pulpy. If you do try it, juice the celery stalks alternately with the tomatoes: the fibrous celery will help push through the tomatoes.

6 ripe tomatoes
3 celery stalks, coarsely chopped
1 garlic clove (optional)
1 red chile, seeded
a dash of Worcestershire sauce
2 measures vodka, or to taste
ice cubes, to serve

SERVES 2

To skin the tomatoes, cut a small cross in the base, put into a large bowl, and cover with boiling water. Leave for 1 minute, then drain and pull off the skins. Put the tomatoes, celery, garlic, if using, chile, Worcestershire sauce, and vodka into a blender and blend until smooth. Pour through a strainer into a pitcher of ice, then serve.

VARIATION *VIRGIN MARY*

Take any classic Bloody Mary recipe and omit the vodka. When you make it with the version above, with fresh tomato juice rather than juice from a bottle or can, it's especially delicious.

bloody mary
with chile vodka

The spicy tastes of traditional Bloody Mary are usually provided by Tabasco sauce. However, you can provide the same spicy flavor by infusing fresh chiles in your bottle of vodka. Test the vodka after 1 day and remove the chile if it's spicy enough. If not, leave for another couple of hours. Take care, and keep tasting, because you can easily make the vodka too hot!

1 cup tomato juice
1 teaspoon Worcestershire sauce
1 tablespoon lemon juice
1 cup crushed ice

to serve
1 lemon wedge
1 celery stalk

chile vodka
1 bottle vodka, 750 ml
2 serrano chiles, halved and seeded

SERVES 1

To make the chile vodka, prick the chiles with a toothpick and gently slide them into the bottle of vodka. Set aside to infuse overnight. Taste, leave longer if liked, then remove and discard the chiles. Keep the vodka in the refrigerator.

To make the Bloody Mary, put the tomato juice into a blender with the Worcestershire sauce, lemon juice, 1 measure of chile vodka, and the crushed ice. Blend well, then pour into tall glasses and serve with a wedge of lemon and celery stalk.

morocco mary

The absolutely best Bloody Mary you ever tasted! I promise you! I have served this recipe to Bloody Mary purists and it was a huge success. In trying to emulate my efforts, one particularly purist friend added the harissa paste to his regular spicy recipe and wondered why some of his guests looked decidedly overheated!

1 teaspoon harissa paste
juice of 2 limes
⅓ cup vodka
1 cup tomato juice
salt and freshly ground black pepper
ice, to serve

SERVES 1–2

Put the harissa, lime juice, and vodka into a pitcher, mix well, then stir in the remaining ingredients.

Alternatively, put the harissa paste, tomato juice, lime juice, vodka, salt, and pepper into a blender and blend well. Pour into a pitcher half-filled with ice and serve.

swedish
glögg

Glögg is the Scandinavian version of Christmas glühwein or mulled wine. (I much prefer it.)

2 bottles dry red wine, 750 ml each

1 bottle aquavit or vodka, 750 ml

12 cardamom pods, crushed

8 whole cloves

1 orange

1 inch fresh ginger, sliced

1 cinnamon stick

1¼ cups sugar

1½ cups blanched almonds

1¼ cups raisins

cinnamon sticks, for stirring (optional)

SERVES ABOUT 20

Using a vegetable peeler or cannelle knife, remove the peel from the orange in a single curl (do not include any of the bitter white pith).

Put everything except the almonds into a large stainless steel or enamel saucepan and set aside overnight (at least 12 hours).

Just before serving, heat to just below boiling point, then remove from the heat and stir in the almonds. Do not let boil or the alcohol will be burned off.

Serve in glass punch cups or tea glasses, with little spoons so people can scoop out the almonds and raisins. Small cinnamon sticks make delicious, scented stirrers.

children's
glögg

Why should children have all the fun? This is wonderful for non-imbibing adults as well.

1 orange

1 quart sweet cider

2 cups apple juice

5 tablespoons sugar

1 cinnamon stick

5 whole cloves

½ cup raisins*

SERVES 10

Using a vegetable peeler or cannelle knife, remove the peel from the orange in a single curl (do not include any of the bitter white pith).

Put the orange peel and all the other ingredients into a large, stainless steel or enamel saucepan. Cover and set aside for 4 hours or overnight.

Just before the party, bring slowly to a boil over a gentle heat, then reduce to low and simmer for 30 minutes. Serve in punch cups or demitasse coffee cups, with some raisins in each serving.

*Note The raisins can be strained out before serving if preferred. Traditionally this recipe also contains slivered almonds: I have omitted them because some children are allergic to nuts.

jamaican
punch

This punch—great for a party—is very
strong, so if you want to give people
more than one glass, make it gentler by
adding a bottle or two of ginger beer,
ginger ale, or sparkling water. If you can't
find ginger wine, use dry sherry, then
add a chunk of fresh ginger, peeled and
finely sliced.

6 limes (3 juiced, 3 sliced)
½ bottle ginger wine, 375 ml
1 bottle white rum or vodka, 750 ml
sugar, to taste
3 lemons, sliced
1 starfruit (carambola), sliced (optional)
1 pineapple, cut lengthwise into long wedges,
    then crosswise into triangles
sprigs of mint, to serve
SERVES ABOUT 16–20

Put the lime juice, ginger wine, rum or vodka, and
sugar into a pitcher and stir until the sugar dissolves.

Fill a punch bowl with ice, add the sliced fruit,
and pour over the ginger wine mixture. Stir well
and serve with sprigs of mint.

caribbean
tea punch

Make this punch with a flavored tea like Lapsang Souchong or Earl Grey. I make mine in a small French press so I can push the plunger as soon as the tea reaches the right color—after 30 seconds to 1 minute, when the color and flavor have developed, but before the bitter tannin is released.

The scent of lemon mixes beautifully with the richness of rum. For parties, make a big pot of tea, mix with half its volume of rum, then sweeten and serve with mixers.

1 cup weak black tea
1 tablespoon sugar
crushed ice
½ cup dark rum or golden rum
peeled zest of ½ lemon
1 slice of lemon (optional)
SERVES 1–2

Stir the sugar into the hot tea. Let cool, then stir well. Fill a glass with crushed ice, pour over the tea, stir in the rum and lemon zest, then serve with a slice of lemon, if using.

mango
rum punch

Many Caribbean punches are very strong, and this is one of them. I also like it turned into a party punch, served in a punch bowl, and topped up with mixers.

1 cup mango purée or 8 oz. frozen mango
1 teaspoon lemon juice
a pinch of ground cardamom*
2 cups golden rum
6 ice cubes
black seeds from 3 green cardamom pods
SERVES 10

Put the mango or mango purée into a blender with the lemon juice, ground cardamom and rum. Add the ice cubes and blend until smooth. Strain into chilled glasses, filled with ice if preferred, and top with a few cardamom seeds, if using.

*Note For the best cardamom, crush 6 green pods with a mortar and pestle, extract the black seeds, and discard the green pods. Grind the pods to a powder using a mortar and pestle.

planter's
punch

There must be hundreds of combinations for Planter's Punch, and their composition probably depended on where the planter lived—this one comes from sugar-growing areas such as Australia and the Caribbean.

1 cup white rum
1 cup pineapple juice (freshly crushed, if possible)
1 cup mango purée or mango juice
grated zest and juice of 1 large lime
a dash of Angostura Bitters
1 cinnamon stick
ice, to serve
SERVES 4–6

Put the rum into a large pitcher, then add the pineapple juice, mango purée or mango juice, the lime zest and juice, and the Bitters. Stir and serve over ice, with a cinnamon swizzle stick.

The daiquiri was born in Cuba and traditionally uses light Cuban rum. It can also be made from a special rum called "shrub," which is also the Hindi word for alcoholic drink.

frozen strawberry
daiquiri

Daiquiris always look so festive, and you can change the fruit to taste: pineapple or banana are both great! I like to use golden rum because it has a better taste, but the color will change somewhat.

juice of 2 limes
2 tablespoons confectioners' sugar
½ cup white rum
6 strawberries
dash of strawberry liqueur (optional)
about 1 cup crushed ice

SERVES 2

Put all the ingredients into a blender and blend until frothy. Pour into chilled daiquiri glasses—preferably enormous!

daiquiri
granita

Put 2 tablespoons sugar syrup and 2 tablespoons lime juice into a blender, add 1½ cups rum, a dash of grenadine, and 1 cup ice, blend until frothy, and serve in chilled glasses. (Sugar syrup is 2–3 parts water mixed with 1 part sugar, boiled for about 2 minutes, then cooled).

Serves 2

lemon-bacardi
daiquiri

Put 3 parts Bacardi into a blender, add 2 parts lemon juice, 1 part sugar syrup, and 1 cup crushed ice. Blend until frothy, then serve in chilled glasses.

Serves 4–5

mint mojito

The Caribbean and Central America have created some fabulous taste combinations, often based on rum.

A mojito is essentially a rum julep, and you can make it in the same way as the Mint Julep on page 116. However, being lazy, I like mine made in a blender, and just love the amazing color produced by the blended mint leaves.

Traditional recipes use club soda as a top-up, but I prefer sparkling water. This is also great without the rum (and without the top-up mixer), but, either way, it's a perfect summer cooler!

½ cup white rum
juice of 1 large lime
¼ cup confectioners' sugar, or to taste
ice cubes
sparkling water or club soda

to serve
leaves from a large bunch of mint, plus extra sprigs
a curl of lime zest
SERVES 1

Put the rum into a blender, add the lime juice, sugar, 4 ice cubes, ½ cup sparkling water, and the mint leaves, and blend until bright green. Strain through a fine strainer into a pitcher, then pour into a tall glass packed with ice. Top with sparkling water or club soda to taste, add the curl of lime zest and a sprig of mint, and serve.

To serve a larger number of people, increase the quantities accordingly, and, instead of pouring into glasses, pour into a pitcher one-third full of ice, then top with sparkling water and serve.

Caribbean mojitos are the coolest of all rum drinks—and I also like them made with tequila. Before serving, strain this drink through a fine strainer to remove the pieces of chopped mint, leaving the liquid a bright, clear, beautiful green.

whiskey

mac

Utterly delicious for people who like their drinks spicy, but not too sweet. For a weaker version, serve in a long glass and top up with a soft drink.

1 measure whiskey
1 measure green ginger wine
ice

to serve
a curl of lemon peel
ginger ale or ginger beer (optional)
SERVES 1

Put the whiskey and ginger wine into a cocktail shaker filled with ice. Shake well, then strain into a small glass and serve with a curl of lemon peel. For a longer drink, top up with ginger ale or ginger beer, if using.

whiskey

sour

I like my sours properly sour, but if you're less adventurous, add a teaspoon of sugar syrup.

¼ cup bourbon or whiskey
the juice of ½ lemon
SERVES 1

Put the bourbon or whiskey into a cocktail shaker filled with ice, shake well, then strain into a whiskey sour glass.

kumquat
ratafia

Kumquats in brandy were a great tradition when I was growing up—no-one could think of anything else to do with the tiny, bitter, jewel-like oranges. Much too strong for children of course, but the adults seemed to love them (I found out why when I grew up).

kumquats, about 1–1½ pints (see method)

sugar (see method)

1 cinnamon stick

3 cloves

brandy (see method)

1-quart preserving jar

MAKES 1 JAR, ABOUT 1 QUART

Wash the kumquats and prick them several times with a skewer or needle. Pack them into the preserving jar and fit crossed bamboo skewers over the top to keep the fruit from rising in the liquid. Fill the jar one-third full with sugar, add the cinnamon and cloves, top up with brandy and set aside for about 2 months.

Serve the liquid as in the previous recipe. The fruit is wonderful sliced and served in fruit puddings, or pan-fried in butter and served with meat or game.

spiced orange
ratafia

grated zest and juice of 6 large oranges

2½ cups sugar

1 cinnamon stick

½ teaspoon ground coriander

1 quart brandy, or enough to fill the jar

2-quart preserving jar

MAKES 1 JAR, ABOUT 2 QUARTS

Put the zest and juice into the preserving jar. Add the sugar, cinnamon stick, and ground coriander.

Stir until the sugar has dissolved and let stand for about 30–60 minutes. Pour over the brandy, cover with a lid, and shake the jar. Set aside for 2 months, shaking the jar from time to time. Serve as a liqueur, poured over ice, or as a long drink with a mixer. I also like this as a sauce for ice cream, sometimes with a light extra sprinkling of finely grated orange zest.

Ratafias are simple to make—just fresh ripe fruits macerated in brandy.

mint julep

Traditionally, a mint julep should be served in a silver or pewter tankard, so the frosty surface isn't marred by finger prints. Tall, frosty glasses, and a drinking straw work just as well.

6 tablespoons sugar syrup

1–1½ cups mint leaves, firmly packed, then torn, plus sprigs of mint

1 teaspoon Angostura Bitters (optional)

1½ cups bourbon

ice cubes

SERVES 6–8

Muddle the sugar syrup in a pitcher with the mint leaves and Bitters, if using. Alternatively, use a mortar and pestle. Stir in the bourbon. Pack a chilled pitcher with ice and mint sprigs, then strain in the julep.

Alternatively, pack tall glasses with ice, then pour over the julep. Serve with straws.

VARIATION *BRANDY MINT JULEP*

Use brandy instead of bourbon and serve as in the main recipe.

mango
and ginger
kir royale

Kir Royale is cassis with champagne. This party drink is based on that idea, and, if you serve it, you won't have to worry about providing anything else. For my mango and ginger version, I use canned Indian Alphonso mango purée when I'm outside mango growing country, and huge ripe Bowen mangoes from Queensland when I'm in Australia. You can also use frozen mango, blended while still frozen to an icy purée. If using fresh or frozen mangoes, you'll have to add a little lemon juice to develop the flavor, and ice to help smash the fibers.

*1 jar preserved stem ginger, about 1 lb., pieces
    cut into quarters, or candied ginger**
2 cups mango purée
½ cup ginger purée or juice*
syrup from the jar of stem ginger (optional)
sugar, to taste
*6 bottles chilled champagne (8 glasses per bottle
    for champagne cocktails)*
MAKES AT LEAST 50 GLASSES

Thread the quarter pieces of ginger, lengthwise, onto the end of a long toothpick or bamboo skewer. Arrange them on a plate or in a bowl, ginger ends downward.

Working in batches if necessary, put the mango purée into a blender, add the ginger purée or juice, the syrup from the jar, if using, and 1 cup ice water. Blend well.

Add sugar to taste. Blend again, then add more ice water until the mixture is the texture of thin cream—if it's too thick it will fall to the bottom of the glass.

Arrange champagne flutes on serving trays, then put 1 teaspoon of the mango mixture into each one. Add a small teaspoon of champagne, stir, and set aside until your guests arrive. When they do, top up the glasses with champagne (twice, because they bubble like mad), then put a ginger toothpick across the top of each one and tell your guests it's a swizzle stick.

They will want more, so have extra mango mixture ready to hand.

*Notes: Preserved stem ginger is sold in Chinatown stores. If unavailable, use candied ginger instead. Ginger purée is sold in jars in some supermarkets. To make your own, cut 2 lb. fresh ginger into pieces about 2 inches long. Soak in water to cover for about 30 minutes, then peel and chop coarsely. Transfer to a blender and work to a purée. You may need to add a little ice water to help the blades run. You can press the juice through a strainer or freeze the pulp in ice cube trays, then use in this and other recipes as needed. You'll need at least 8 cubes for this recipe.

rosa-
frizzare

A refreshing combination from Southern Italy. Mix ½ cup Campari and 1½ cups grapefruit juice in a pitcher. To serve, half-fill each glass with the mixture, add ice, and top up with champagne. For a special party, decorate with sprigs of mint.
Serves 6

mandarin
fizz

Mix 1 quart mandarin juice and 1 cup Cointreau or Grand Marnier in a chilled pitcher.

To serve, pour a little of the mixture into each glass, then top with champagne.

For a single cocktail, omit the champagne and pour the fiery juice over ice.
Serves 12–16

bellini
kir

Put about 2 tablespoons peach liqueur and some sliced peach into each champagne glass and top with chilled champagne or other sparkling wine.
Serves 1 or many

I created the Mango and Ginger Kir Royale (a Southeast Asian version of a traditional Provençal Kir Royale) to serve at a book launch. I knew I was onto a winner when we just couldn't keep up with the demand. Try it at your next party.

champagne
cocktail

This delicious champagne cocktail is also a variation on the popular Kir Royale.

1 teaspoon of a liqueur such as Poire William, peach or strawberry liqueur, framboise, Midori, blue curaçao, or Galliano (if using Galliano, add the pulp and seeds of 1 passionfruit)
alternatively, ¼ cup fruit juice, such as pear, pineapple, peach, or apricot
1 shot of vodka (optional)
champagne or other sparkling wine

SERVES 1

Put 1 teaspoon of liqueur or ¼ cup fruit juice into a champagne flute or coupé, add the vodka, if using, and top up with champagne.

For extra pizzazz, decorate the glass with a fine slice of the fruit used to make the liqueur.

blue
champagne

Spectacularly chic, this is one you should only serve if you're prepared for your guests to be merry in a matter of seconds. Serve to the firstcomers—otherwise everyone will want one!

2 teaspoons freshly squeezed lemon juice
½ teaspoon Triple Sec or Cointreau*
½ teaspoon blue curaçao
½ cup vodka
champagne or other sparkling wine

SERVES 2

Put ice cubes into a cocktail shaker, then add the lemon juice, Triple Sec or Cointreau, curaçao, and vodka.

Shake, then strain into 2 champagne flutes and top up with champagne.

*Note Triple Sec is best, but can be difficult to find. Use any dry orange-flavored liqueur instead—Cointreau is the most common.

Champagne is the great party drink and champagne cocktails are equally popular: make them with fruit purées, added liquor, or liqueurs—all delicious.

This traditional English summertime drink is perfect for tennis parties and polo matches. When the borage herb is in flower, freeze the pretty blue blossoms in ice cubes for out-of-season drinks.

pimms

Allow 1 cup per drink, and at least 2 drinks per person if serving Pimms for a party and be prepared for repeat orders! The cucumber is mandatory—somehow it wouldn't be Pimms without it. Look out for the small cucumbers shown on this page—you can cut them lengthwise to make pretty shapes. Take care—this delicious cooler tastes heavenly, but is deceptively strong.

1 part Pimms
3 parts ginger ale, lemonade, lemon soda,
  or club soda
borage flowers
curls of cucumber peel
sliced lemons and sprigs of mint
SERVES 1 OR A PARTY

Put all the ingredients into a pitcher of ice, stir well, and serve.

ruby grapefruit campari

Wonderful for a summer party—serve one tall glass per person as a welcoming drink. Campari at this level of dilution isn't very intoxicating, so this is a perfect drink for early in the day and absolutely gorgeous for brunch parties.

1 quart ruby grapefruit juice, chilled
½ cup Campari, or to taste
1 cup crushed ice
sprigs of mint, to serve

SERVES 8–10

Put the grapefruit juice, Campari, and crushed ice into a blender and blend briefly.

Half-fill a pitcher with more crushed ice and cram lots of mint sprigs into the pitcher. Pour the Campari mixture over the top, then serve.

index

picture credits and acknowledgments

William Lingwood (from *Fingerfood, Juices and Tonics, and A Handful of Herbs*)
p. 3–5, p. 9, p. 12–13, p. 18–19, p. 22–25, p. 30–31,
p. 36–37, p. 42–44, p.46–47, p. 50–51, p. 54–59,
p. 61–74, p. 76–77, p. 80–81, p.83, p. 86–87, p. 90–94,
p. 100–103, p. 110–111, p. 115, p. 118–122

James Merrell (from *Coolers and Summer Cocktails* and
Smoothies and Other Blended Drinks) p. 1–2, p. 6–7,
p. 15, p. 21, p. 27–28, p. 33–35, p. 38–40, p. 45, p. 48,
p. 52–53, p. 60, p. 75, p. 78, p. 82, p. 84, p. 88–89,
p. 95–96, p. 99, p. 104–109, p. 112–114, p. 116–117,
p. 123–125, p.128

Debi Treloar (from *Smoothies and Shakes* and *Soda
Fountain Classics*) p. 11, p. 16–17, p. 41

Pia Tryde (from *Pure Style Outdoors*) p. 98

Christopher Drake (from *Open Air Living*) p. 20, p. 97

conversion chart

Weights and measures have been rounded up or down slightly to make measuring easier.

weight equivalents:

imperial	metric
1 oz.	25 g
2 oz.	50 g
3 oz.	75 g
4 oz.	125 g
5 oz.	150 g
6 oz.	175 g
7 oz.	200 g
8 oz. (1/2 lb.)	250 g
9 oz.	275 g
10 oz.	300 g
11 oz.	325 g
12 oz.	375 g
13 oz.	400 g
14 oz.	425 g
15 oz.	475 g
16 oz. (1 lb.)	500 g
2 lb.	1 kg

measurements:

inches	cm
1/4 inch	5 mm
1/2 inch	1 cm
3/4 inch	1.5 cm
1 inch	2.5 cm
2 inches	5 cm
3 inches	7 cm
4 inches	10 cm
5 inches	12 cm
6 inches	15 cm
7 inches	18 cm
8 inches	20 cm
9 inches	23 cm
10 inches	25 cm
11 inches	28 cm
12 inches	30 cm

oven temperatures:

225°F	110°C	Gas 1/4
250°F	120°C	Gas 1/2
275°F	140°C	Gas 1
300°F	150°C	Gas 2
325°F	160°C	Gas 3
350°F	180°C	Gas 4
375°F	190°C	Gas 5
400°F	200°C	Gas 6
425°F	220°C	Gas 7
450°F	230°C	Gas 8
475°F	240°C	Gas 9

volume equivalents

american	metric	imperial
1 teaspoon	5 ml	
1 tablespoon	15 ml	
1/4 cup	60 ml	2 fl.oz.
1/3 cup	75 ml	2 1/2 fl.oz.
1/2 cup	125 ml	4 fl.oz.
2/3 cup	150 ml	5 fl.oz. (1/4 pint)
3/4 cup	175 ml	6 fl.oz.
1 cup	250 ml	8 fl.oz.

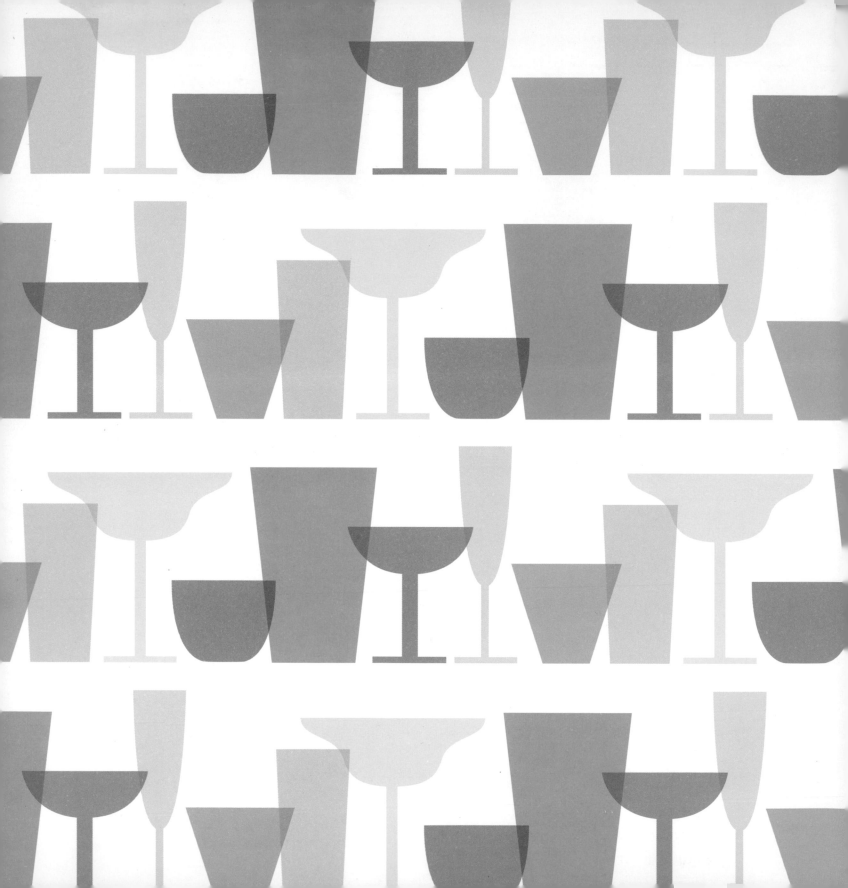